# The Songs of
# GEORGE & IRA GERSHWIN ®

## A
## CENTENNIAL CELEBRATION

GERSHWIN® and GEORGE GERSHWIN®
are registered trademarks of Gershwin Enterprises
IRA GERSHWIN™ is a trademark of Gershwin Enterprises
PORGY AND BESS® is a registered trademark of Porgy And Bess Enterprises
CRAZY FOR YOU® is a registered trademark of Crazy For You Enterprises
All Rights Reserved

All Photos courtesy of Ira and Leonore Gershwin Trusts
Project Manager: Sy Feldman
Compiled and Edited by Tony Esposito
Interior Art Layout: Odalis Soto

**WARNER BROS. PUBLICATIONS - THE GLOBAL LEADER IN PRINT**
**USA:** 15800 NW 48th Avenue, Miami, FL 33014

 **WARNER/CHAPPELL MUSIC**

 Carisch **NUOVA CARISCH**

**IMP** **INTERNATIONAL MUSIC PUBLICATIONS LIMITED**

**CANADA:** 40 SHEPPARD AVE. WEST, SUITE 800
TORONTO, ONTARIO, M2N 6K9
**SCANDINAVIA:** P.O. BOX 533, VENDEVAGEN 85 B
S-182 15, DANDERYD, SWEDEN
**AUSTRALIA:** P.O. BOX 353
3 TALAVERA ROAD, NORTH RYDE N.S.W. 2113

**ITALY:** VIA CAMPANIA, 12
20098 S. GIULIANO MILANESE (MI)
ZONA INDUSTRIALE SESTO ULTERIANO
**SPAIN:** MAGALLANES, 25
28015 MADRID
**FRANCE:** 25 RUE DE HAUTEVILLE, 75010 PARIS

**ENGLAND:** SOUTHEND ROAD,
WOODFORD GREEN, ESSEX IG8 8HN
**GERMANY:** MARSTALLSTR. 8, D-80539 MUNCHEN
**DENMARK:** DANMUSIK, VOGNMAGERGADE 7
DK 1120 KOBENHAVNK

# Contents

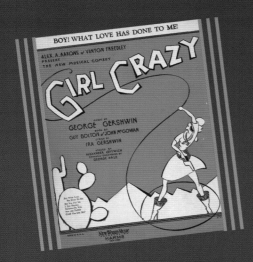

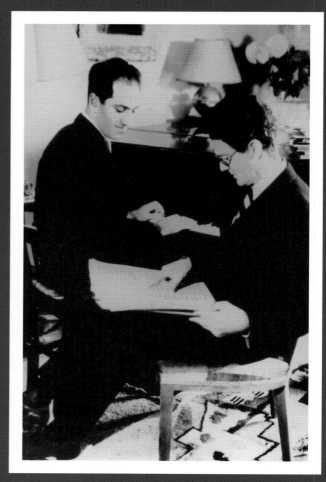

George Gershwin with William M. Daly
circa 1932

George Gershwin, Guy Bolton
and Ira Gershwin
1930

Oscar Levant, Otto Langley, George Gershwin, Robert Russell Bennett, Fritz Reiner, Deems Taylor and
Bill Daly at Lewisohn Stadium, NYC at rehearsal for "All American Concert"
Aug. 1931

George Gershwin with Serge Koussevitzky
publicity for "Second Rhapsody"
1932

Ira, Frances, George and Arthur Gershwin
1933

George Gershwin, NYC
1933

"Ira" by George

George Gershwin writing last note of
"Porgy and Bess"
1935

George Gershwin with cast of "Porgy and Bess"
Alvin Theater, NYC
1935

"Porgy and Bess"
1935

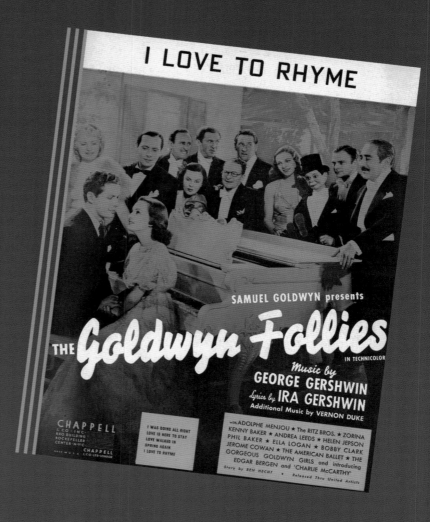

George Gershwin
1936

George Gershwin
1934

George Gershwin, DuBose Heyward and Ira Gershwin
1935

All Gershwin Concert
Philharmonic Auditorium, Los Angeles
1937

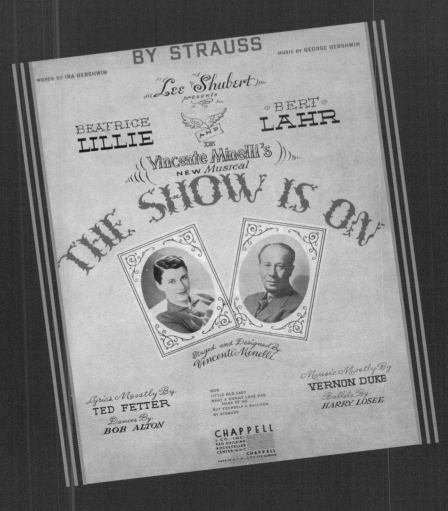

George and Ira Gershwin
arriving at LAX
1936

**George Gershwin
conducting RKO Orchestra for
"Shall We Dance"
1937**

**George Gershwin
on set of "Shall We Dance"
1936**

Ira Gershwin at work, NYC
1938

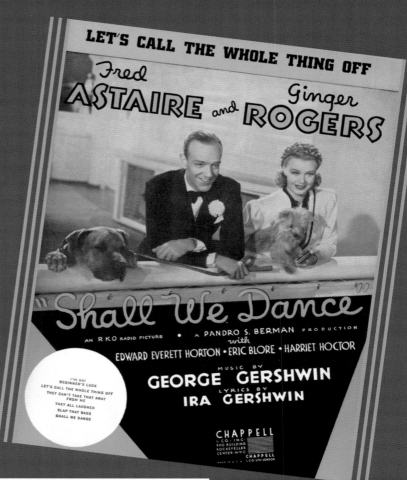

Hermes Pan, Fred Astaire, Ginger Rogers, Mark Sandrich,
George Gershwin, Ira Gershwin and Nat Shilkret on the set of "Shall We Dance"
1936

Ira Gershwin, Beverly Hills, CA
1952

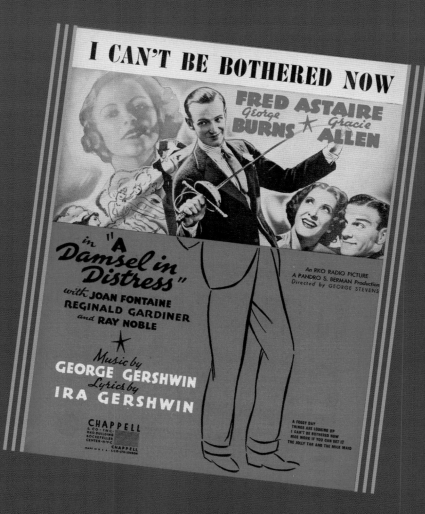

# DO WHAT YOU DO!

Music and Lyrics by
GEORGE GERSHWIN,
IRA GERSHWIN and GUS KAHN

I nev-er knew__ love was so nice,__ I nev-er kissed__ an-y-one twice,__ { I nev-er want-ed a beau. } { my heart was nev-er a-glow. } Poor me! I just did—n't know. You came a-long,__

Do What You Do! - 4 - 1

# Feeling Sentimental

Music and Lyrics by
GEORGE GERSHWIN,
IRA GERSHWIN and GUS KAHN

Feeling Sentimental - 4 - 1

# HARLEM SERENADE

Music and Lyrics by
**GEORGE GERSHWIN,**
**IRA GERSHWIN and GUS KAHN**

**Allegretto moderato**

From the Con - go jun - gle it came, a rhy - thm set - ting Har - lem a - flame, hear it once, you're nev - er the same, I'm re - fer - ring to the Har - lem Ser - e - nade. New kind o' mu - sic and

new kind o' time, new kind o' rhy - thm and new kind o' rhyme,

I have seen a - gain____ and a - gain the san - est of men go daf -

- fy - dil when it's played.____

*Refrain:*

Take a tax - i and go there; you'll meet peo - ple you

# I Must Be Home by Twelve O'Clock

Music and Lyrics by
GEORGE GERSHWIN,
IRA GERSHWIN and GUS KAHN

# LIZA
## (All The Clouds'll Roll Away)

Music and Lyrics by
GEORGE GERSHWIN,
IRA GERSHWIN and GUS KAHN

Moon shin-in' on the riv - er Come a - long, my Li - za! Breeze sing - in' through the tree - tops Come a - long, my Li - za! Some-thin' might-y sweet I want to

Liza - 4 - 1

# SO ARE YOU!

Music and Lyrics by
**GEORGE GERSHWIN,
IRA GERSHWIN and GUS KAHN**

When a fel-la tries to tell a girl what's in his heart, he'd save a lot of time if he could on-ly rhyme. Ev-'ry girl loves hear-ing her love speak with po-et's art.

So Are You! - 4 - 1

# TONIGHT'S THE NIGHT

Music and Lyrics by
GEORGE GERSHWIN,
IRA GERSHWIN and GUS KAHN

I've just got a feel-ing to-night's the night,—

— let's tear down the ceil-ing, to-

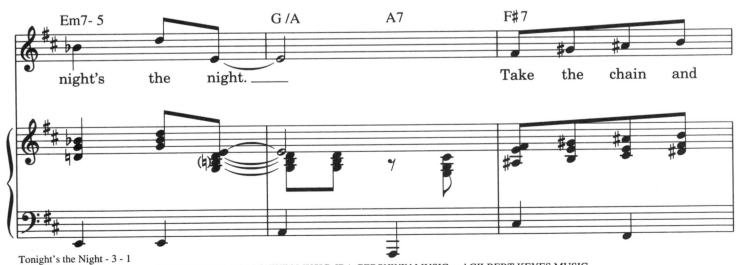

night's the night.—— Take the chain and

Tonight's the Night - 3 - 1

# IN THE MANDARIN'S ORCHID GARDEN

Music and Lyrics by
**GEORGE GERSHWIN**
and **IRA GERSHWIN**

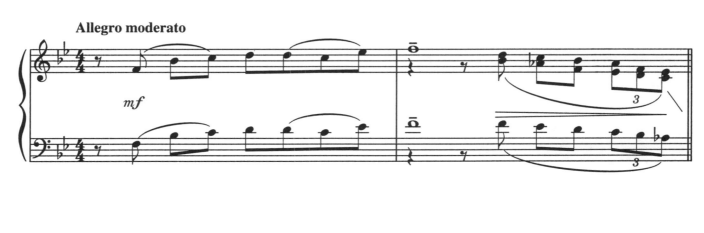

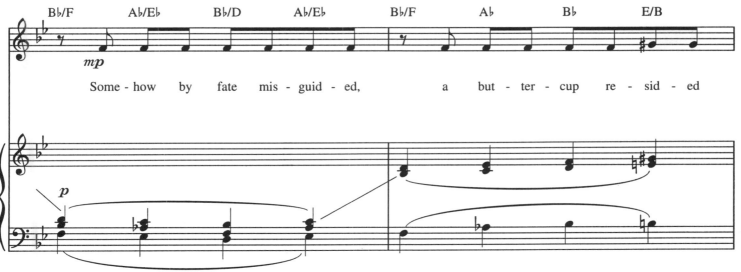

Some - how by fate mis - guid - ed, a but - ter - cup re - sid - ed

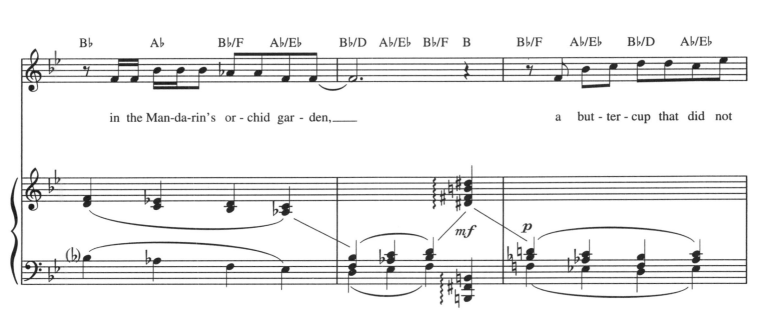

in the Man - da - rin's or - chid gar - den,____ a but - ter - cup that did not

In the Mandarin's Orchid Garden - 5 - 1

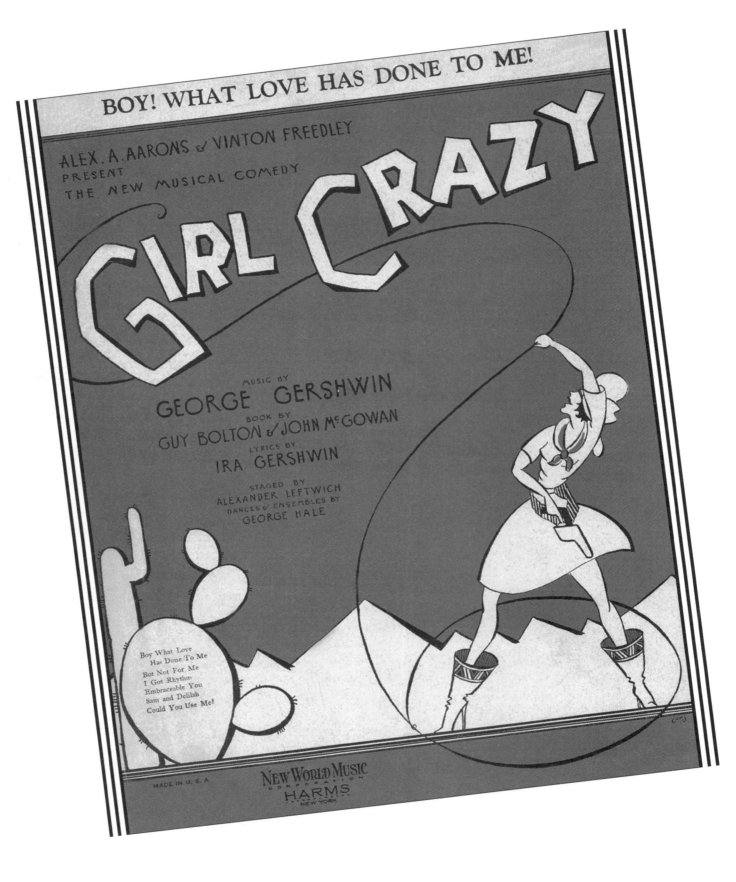

# BARBARY COAST

Music and Lyrics by
GEORGE GERSHWIN
and IRA GERSHWIN

Barbary Coast - 4 - 1

# BIDIN' MY TIME

Music and Lyrics by
GEORGE GERSHWIN
and IRA GERSHWIN

**Moderato**

**Gracefully**

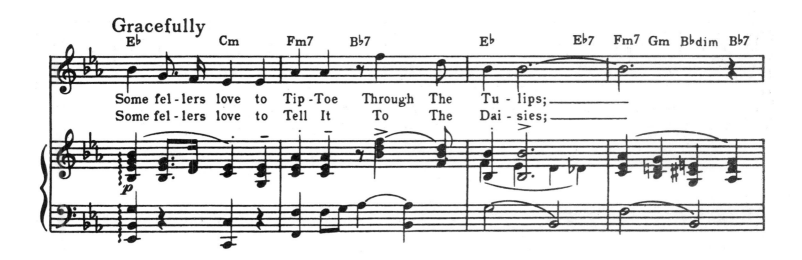

Some fel-lers love to Tip-Toe Through The Tu-lips;
Some fel-lers love to Tell It To The Dai-sies;

Some fel-lers go on Sing - ing In The Rain.
Some Stroll Be-neath The Hon - ey-suc-kle Vines;

Bidin' My Time - 3 - 1

# BOY! WHAT LOVE HAS DONE TO ME!

Music and Lyrics by
GEORGE GERSHWIN
and IRA GERSHWIN

Boy! What Love Has Done to Me! - 5 - 1

Rather slow (sorrowfully)

Refrain:

1. I fetch his slip - pers; fill up the pipe he smokes. I cook the kip - pers;
2. See additional lyrics

58

*Second Refrain:*
His brains are minus,
Never a thought in sight—
And yet his highness
Lectures me day and night;
Oh, where was my sense
To sign that wedding license?
Boy! What love had done to me!

My life he's wrecking;
Bet you could find him now
Out somewhere necking
Somebody else's frau.
You get to know life
When married to a low-life—
Boy! What love has done to me!

I can't hold my head up:
The butcher, the baker,
All know he's a faker;
Brother, I am fed up—
But if I left him he'd be up a tree.

Where will I wind up?
I don't know where I'm at.
I make my mind up
I ought to leave him flat.
But I have grown so
I love the dirty so'n'so!
Boy! What love has done to me!

# BRONCHO BUSTERS

Music and Lyrics by
GEORGE GERSHWIN
and IRA GERSHWIN

town we used to fret a - way un - til we made our get a - way, out
won - der - ful to breeze a - round, they seem to have real trees a - round, and

here, where there's no doubt that men are men,_____ where men_____
of the o - pen spac - es there's no doubt,_____ no doubt,_____

Broncho Busters - 7 - 1

62

They sling a line that does a girl no good.

*(Cowboys march on)*

Cowboys:

We're

bron - cho bust - ers, we bust the bron - chos, we nev - er fear

Broncho Busters - 7 - 4

# BUT NOT FOR ME

Music and Lyrics by
GEORGE GERSHWIN
and IRA GERSHWIN

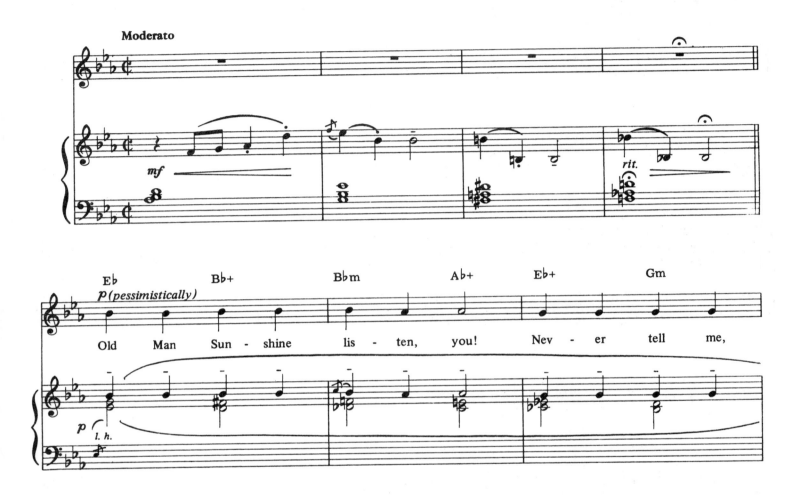

But Not for Me - 4 - 1

But Not for Me - 4 - 2

# (When It's) CACTUS TIME IN ARIZONA

Music and Lyrics by
GEORGE GERSHWIN
and IRA GERSHWIN

# COULD YOU USE ME?

Music and Lyrics by
GEORGE GERSHWIN
and IRA GERSHWIN

Danny: Have some pit - y on an East - ern - er;
Ginger: There's a chap I know in Mex - i - co,

Show a lit - tle sym - pa - thy;
Who's as strong as he can be;

No one pos - sib - ly could
Eat - ing nails and drink - ing

be stern - er
Tex - a - co

Than you have been with me.
He is the type for me.

There's a job that I'm ap-
There is one in Cal - i -

Could You Use Me? - 4 - 1

I'm no Elk or Mas-on or Wood-man, Who gets home at three. The
Could you warm me up in a bliz-zard, Say, for-ty be - low? Your

girls who see_ me Grow soft and dream-y, But I'm a gan - der who
ties are freak-ish; Your knees look weak-ish, Go back to flap - pers And

won't phil-an - der, Oh, could you use_ me? Cause I cer-tain-ly could use
high - ball lap - pers! Though you can use_ me, I most cer-tain-ly can't use

1.
you!_____

2.
Oh,
For,
you!_____

# EMBRACEABLE YOU

Music and Lyrics by
GEORGE GERSHWIN
and IRA GERSHWIN

He: Doz-ens of girls would storm up, I had to lock my door.
She: I went a-bout re-cit-ing, "Here's one who'll nev-er fall!"

Some-how I could-n't warm up To one be-fore.
But I'm a-fraid the writ-ing Is on the wall.

Embraceable You - 4 - 1

Embraceable You - 4 - 3

# I Got Rhythm

Music and Lyrics by
GEORGE GERSHWIN
and IRA GERSHWIN

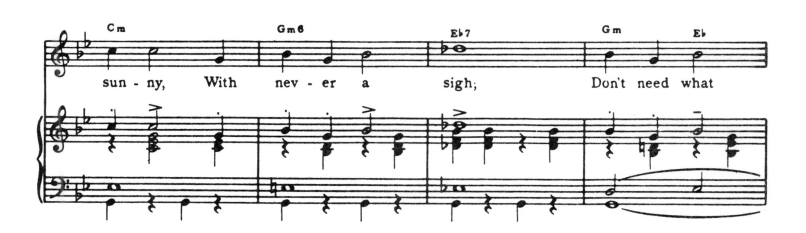

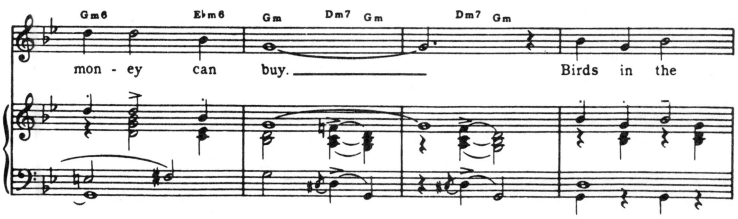

I Got Rhythm - 4 - 1

84

# Sam and Delilah

Music and Lyrics by
GEORGE GERSHWIN
and IRA GERSHWIN

De - li - lah___ was a flooz - y,___

she nev - er___ gave a damn;___

Sam and Delilah - 6 - 1

It's al - ways that way with pas - sion, so cow-boy, learn to be -

have, or else you're li - 'ble to cash in

with no tomb - stone on your grave.

**Broad** *Kate and ensemble*

De - li - lah, oh! De - li - lah,

*ben marcato*

# TREAT ME ROUGH

Music and Lyrics by
GEORGE GERSHWIN
and IRA GERSHWIN

When I was born, they found a sil-ver spoon in my mouth;— I had a bar-ber just to curl my hair._____ If win-ter came, the ma-ter car-ried me to the South;— the point is that I had the best of care._____ Wom-en and head-wait-ers fawned on me.__

Treat Me Rough - 3 - 1

# You've Got What Gets Me

Music and Lyrics by
GEORGE GERSHWIN
and IRA GERSHWIN

I've got a se-cret that I can con-ceal no long - er,____

____ And you're the one that I sim-ply must tell it

You've Got What Gets Me - 4 - 1

Refrain

You've got what gets me, What gets me you've got;—

You've got what gets me, I don't know just what.— But when you

smile on me— I get proud-er and proud-er; My heart goes

on a spree,— Beat-ing loud-er and loud-er. You've got what

You've Got What Gets Me - 4 - 4

# BLAH-BLAH-BLAH

Music and Lyrics by
GEORGE GERSHWIN
and IRA GERSHWIN

Moderato

writ-ten you a song, A beau-ti-ful rou-tine; (I hope you

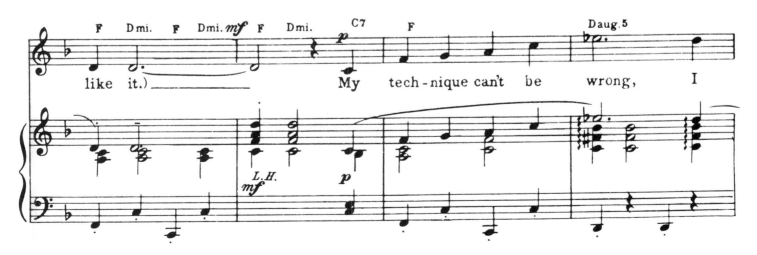

like it.) My tech-nique can't be wrong, I

Blah-Blah-Blah - 4 - 1

# DELISHIOUS

Music and Lyrics by
GEORGE GERSHWIN
and IRA GERSHWIN

What can I say___ To sing my praise of you?___ I must re-

veal _____ The things I feel.___ What can I say?___ Each love-ly

Delishious - 4 - 1

# KATINKITSCHKA

Music and Lyrics by
GEORGE GERSHWIN
and IRA GERSHWIN

Allegretto giocoso

(Popitschka and Momitschka sing:
Katinka pantomimes)

Ka -
Ka -

tink - itsch - ka, Ka - tink - itsch - ka, out all night long! Ka -
tink - itsch - ka, Ka - tink - itsch - ka, oh, what a dis - grace! Ka -

Katinkitschka - 3 - 1

*Refrain:*

Pop - itsch - ka, Mom - itsch - ka will not sleep a wink - itsch - ka,
Pop - itsch - ka, Mom - itsch - ka now can laugh and sing - itsch - ka,

Pop - itsch - ka, Mom - itsch - ka will not sleep a wink - itsch - ka.
Pop - itsch - ka, Mom - itsch - ka now can laugh and sing - itsch - ka.

*(The three join hands and romp)*

Think - ing of Ka - tink, Ka - tink, Ka - tink, Ka - tink, Ka - tink - itsch - ka!
Since Ka - tink, Ka - tink, Ka - tink - a has a wed - ding ring - itsch - ka!

**Allegro**
*Dance*

# Somebody From Somewhere

Music and Lyrics by
GEORGE GERSHWIN
and IRA GERSHWIN

When a bod-y knows no-bod-y, what's a bod-y to do?

Shall she weep and sigh? No, no, and I'll tell you why:

Somebody From Somewhere - 3 - 1

# BECAUSE, BECAUSE

Music and Lyrics by
GEORGE GERSHWIN
and IRA GERSHWIN

Because, Because - 4 - 1

# THE ILLEGITIMATE DAUGHTER

Music and Lyrics by
GEORGE GERSHWIN
and IRA GERSHWIN

*(French Ambassador to the President)*

You have done a great in-

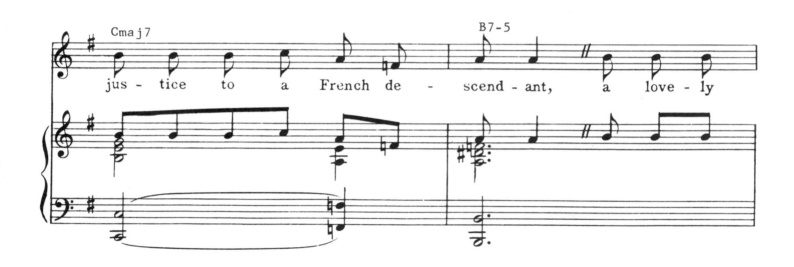

jus - tice to a French de - scend - ant, a love - ly

girl, Whose rights have been tram - pled in the dust.

The Illegitimate Daughter - 5 - 1

# A Kiss for Cinderella

Music and Lyrics by
GEORGE GERSHWIN
and IRA GERSHWIN

*Wintergreen:* But on this glo-rious day I find I'm sen-ti-men-tal-ly in-clined, and so I sing this to the girls I used to know: Here's a kiss for Cin-der-el-la and a part-ing kiss for May, too-dle-

# LOVE IS SWEEPING THE COUNTRY

Music and Lyrics by
GEORGE GERSHWIN
and IRA GERSHWIN

Love Is Sweeping the Country - 4 - 1

# OF THEE I SING
## (Baby)

Music and Lyrics by
GEORGE GERSHWIN
and IRA GERSHWIN

From the Is - land of Man - hat - tan to the Coast of Gold, From North to

South, From East to West, You are the love I love the best.

Of Thee I Sing - 4 - 1

Of thee I sing, ba-by, You have got that cer-tain thing, ba-by! Shin-ing star and in-spi-ra-tion Worth-y of a might-y na-tion Of thee I sing.

# The Senator From Minnesota

Music and Lyrics by
GEORGE GERSHWIN
and IRA GERSHWIN

The Senator From Minnesota - 4 - 1

The Senator From Minnesota - 4 - 3

# WHO CARES?
## (So Long As You Care for Me)

Music and Lyrics by
GEORGE GERSHWIN
and IRA GERSHWIN

Let it rain and thun-der! Let a mil-lion

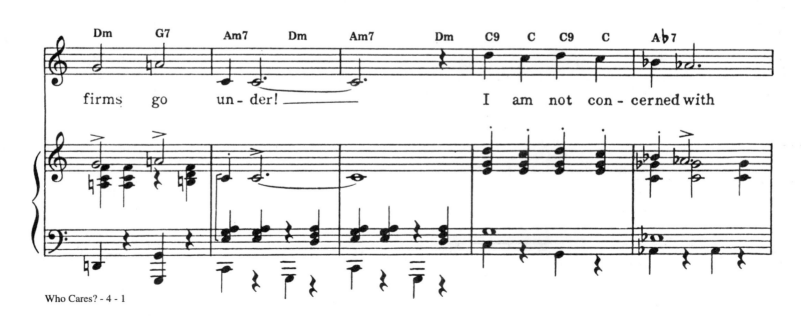

firms go un-der! I am not con-cerned with

Who Cares? - 4 - 1

# WINTERGREEN FOR PRESIDENT

Music and Lyrics by
GEORGE GERSHWIN
and IRA GERSHWIN

# Isn't It a Pity?

Music and Lyrics by
**GEORGE GERSHWIN**
and **IRA GERSHWIN**

*Michael:* Why did I wan - der, here and there and yon - der,
*Ilse:* While you were flit - ting I was bus - y knit - ting,

wast - ing pre - cious time for no rea - son or
hop - ing I'd sur - vive, hop - ing you'd ar -

# I'VE GOT TO BE THERE

Music and Lyrics by
**GEORGE GERSHWIN**
and **IRA GERSHWIN**

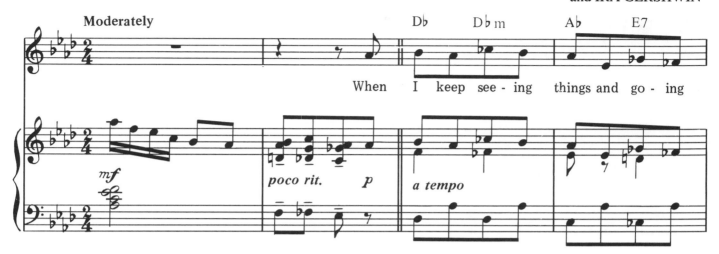

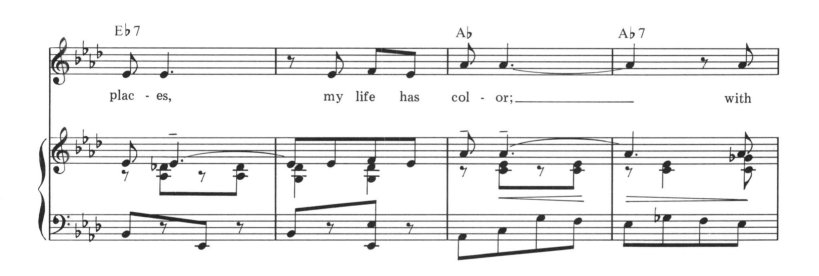

I've Got to Be There - 4 - 1

When - ev - er peo - ple step up to say, "Let's step to - night," if

I've been low I pep up; a - gain the fut - ure's bright! When -

ev - er there's a par - ty I can go to, it makes the

world seem right! _____ When

I've Got to Be There - 4 - 2

*Refrain*

Ab     Eb7     B°7     F7/C     Bb m7-5

mus - ic is play - ing and coup - les are sway - ing, say! I've got to be

Ab     Eb7     Ab     Eb7     Ab     Eb7

there! I've got to be there! When joy's in the mak - ing and

B°7     F7/C     Bb m7-5     Ab     Eb7

ceil - ings are shak - ing, and there's nev-er a care, I've got to be

Ab     C7     F7

there! Check my hat, and throw the stub a - way!

I've Got to Be There - 4 - 3

# THE LORELEI

Music and Lyrics by
GEORGE GERSHWIN
and IRA GERSHWIN

The Lorelei - 4 - 1

# LUCKIEST MAN IN THE WORLD

Music and Lyrics by
GEORGE GERSHWIN
and IRA GERSHWIN

# MY COUSIN IN MILWAUKEE

Music and Lyrics by
GEORGE GERSHWIN
and IRA GERSHWIN

Once I vis-i-ted My Cous-in,___ In Mil-wau-kee, U. S. A., She got boy-friends by the doz-en ___ When she

My Cousin in Milwaukee - 5 - 1

# SO WHAT?

Music and Lyrics by
GEORGE GERSHWIN
and IRA GERSHWIN

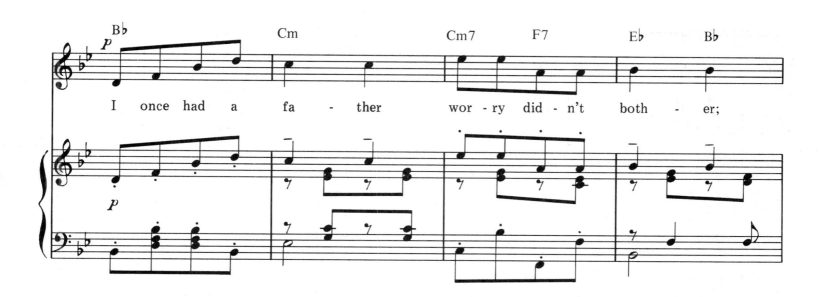

I once had a fa - ther wor -ry did -n't both - er;

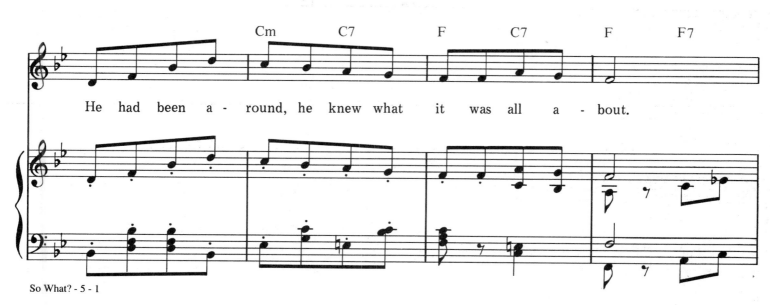

He had been a - round, he knew what it was all a - bout.

So What? - 5 - 1

# Where You Go, I Go

Music and Lyrics by
GEORGE GERSHWIN
and IRA GERSHWIN

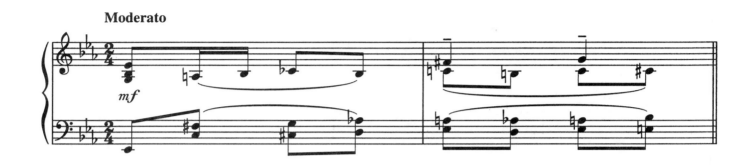

*Bauer:* La - dy, let me go! I want to say good - bye. *Gita:* My

lov - er, don't you know I'm yours un - til I die?

Where You Go, I Go - 4 - 1

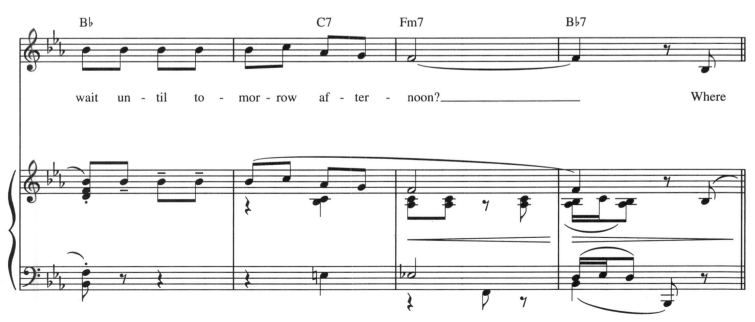

178

Refrain:

you go, I go, 'cause I wan-na go where you go!
you go, I go, 'cause I wan-na go where you go!

Oh! My hon - ey! Love is so fun - ny! Where
If you crave me, no one can save me. Where

you flee, I flee, 'cause I wan-na fly where you flee!
you flee, I flee, 'cause I wan-na fly where you flee!

I've got to fol - low when you call._____
I see the writ - ing on the wall._____

Where You Go, I Go - 4 - 3

ON AND ON AND ON
Reference Copy,
SAM H. HARRIS
PRESENTS
Let 'Em Eat Cake
LYRICS BY
IRA GERSHWIN
MUSIC BY
GEORGE GERSHWIN
BOOK BY
GEORGE S. KAUFMAN
AND
MORRIE RYSKIND
DIRECTED BY
GEORGE S. KAUFMAN
DANCES AND ENSEMBLES BY
VON GRONA
AND
NED McGURN
Union Square
On And On And On
Let 'Em Eat Cake
Mine
NEW WORLD MUSIC CORPORATION
HARMS INCORPORATED
NEW YORK
MADE IN U.S.A.
harris

# BLUE, BLUE, BLUE

Music and Lyrics by
GEORGE GERSHWIN
and IRA GERSHWIN

Blue, Blue, Blue - 3 - 2

# LET 'EM EAT CAKE

Music and Lyrics by
GEORGE GERSHWIN
and IRA GERSHWIN

Let 'Em Eat Cake - 5 - 1

# MINE

Music and Lyrics by
**GEORGE GERSHWIN**
**and IRA GERSHWIN**

Mine - 7 - 1

Mine - 7 - 3

192

Mine - 7 - 4

*(1st time counter-melody alone, 2nd time both melodies)*

2nd Refrain:

Mine, _____ love is mine, _____

Patter

The point they're mak - ing in the song _____ Is that they more than

Wheth - er it's rain or storm or

get a - long, _ And he is not a - shamed to say _

shine. _____ Mine, _____ you are mine, _

She made him what he is to - day. _ It does a per - son good to see _

*grazioso e leggiero*

Mine - 7 - 5

# ON AND ON AND ON

Music and Lyrics by
GEORGE GERSHWIN
and IRA GERSHWIN

Left! Right! Left! Right! Left! Right! Left! Right! March-ing, march-ing all the

time. Hep, hep, hep, hep, Thru ev-'ry kind of scen-e-ry and

On and on and On - 4 - 1

Refrain
Tempo di Marcia

On! And on! And on! _____ Hith-er and thith-er and yon! _____ It seems to be the thing For march-ing men to sing. On! And on! And on! So on! And on! And on! _____

On and on and On - 4 - 4

# UNION SQUARE

Music and Lyrics by
GEORGE GERSHWIN
and IRA GERSHWIN

Moderato con moto

*Refrain:*

Our hearts are in com-mun-ion, when we gath-er down in Un-ion Square, heigh - ho! When whisk-ers are un-shav-en, one can al-ways find a hav-en there, heigh ho! Though some may pre-fer the charm-ing Bron-nix, though some sing of daint-y Sut-ton Place, 'tis here we dis-cov-er all the

Union Square - 7 - 1

Our hearts are in com-mun-ion when we gath-er down in Un-ion Square, heigh-

ho! When whisk-ers are un-shav-en, one can al-ways find a hav-en there, heigh-

ho! Though some may pre-fer the charm-ing Bron-nix, though some sing of daint-y Sut-ton

Place, 'tis here we dis-cov-er all the ton-ics that

# TILL THEN

Music and Lyrics by
GEORGE GERSHWIN
and IRA GERSHWIN

ev - er and a day is a long time," I've heard it said, but, is it

true? For - ev - er and a day is a song time, if I can

Till Then - 4 - 1

Till Then - 4 - 3

# Bess, You Is My Woman Now

From *Porgy and Bess* ®
By GEORGE GERSHWIN,
DU BOSE and DOROTHY HEYWARD
and IRA GERSHWIN

Bess, You Is My Woman Now - 8 - 1

Bess, You Is My Woman Now - 8 - 2

Bess, You Is My Woman Now - 8 - 4

Bess, You Is My Woman Now - 8 - 6

Bess, You Is My Woman Now - 8 - 8

# I Got Plenty o' Nuttin'

From *Porgy and Bess* ®
By GEORGE GERSHWIN,
DU BOSE and DOROTHY HEYWARD
and IRA GERSHWIN

# I Loves You, Porgy

From *Porgy and Bess* ®
By GEORGE GERSHWIN,
DU BOSE and DOROTHY HEYWARD
and IRA GERSHWIN

I Loves You, Porgy - 5 - 1

**Più appassionato, ma ben ritmato**

*Bess:* I loves you, Por - gy,_____ don' let him

*Porgy:* Bess, _____ what you think I is an - y - way, to let that

take me,_____ don' let him han-dle me_____ with his hot

dirt - y houn' dog steal my wom-an?_____ If you wants to stay wid Por - gy, you go - in'

# It Ain't Necessarily So

From *Porgy and Bess* ®
By GEORGE GERSHWIN,
DU BOSE and DOROTHY HEYWARD
and IRA GERSHWIN

It Ain't Necessarily So - 6 - 1

It Ain't Necessarily So - 6 - 2

# Oh Bess, Oh Where's My Bess

From *Porgy and Bess* ®
By GEORGE GERSHWIN,
DU BOSE and DOROTHY HEYWARD
and IRA GERSHWIN

# THERE'S A BOAT DAT'S LEAVIN' SOON FOR NEW YORK

From *Porgy and Bess* ®
By GEORGE GERSHWIN,
DU BOSE and DOROTHY HEYWARD
and IRA GERSHWIN

There's a Boat Dat's Leavin' Soon for New York - 4 - 1

There's a Boat Dat's Leavin' Soon for New York - 4 - 3

# BY STRAUSS

Music and Lyrics by
GEORGE GERSHWIN
and IRA GERSHWIN

Tempo di Valse Viennoise

A - way with the mu - sic of Broad- way! _____ Be off with your Irv - ing Ber - lin! _____

By Strauss - 5 - 1

By Strauss - 5 - 2

# HI-HO!

Music and Lyrics by
**GEORGE GERSHWIN**
and **IRA GERSHWIN**

Hi-Ho! - 8 - 1

# (I've Got) BEGINNER'S LUCK

Music and Lyrics by
GEORGE GERSHWIN
and IRA GERSHWIN

(I've Got) Beginner's Luck - 4 - 1

(I've Got) Beginner's Luck - 4 - 3

(I've Got) Beginner's Luck - 4 - 4

# LET'S CALL THE WHOLE THING OFF

Music and Lyrics by
**GEORGE GERSHWIN**
**and IRA GERSHWIN**

Let's Call the Whole Thing Off - 6 - 1

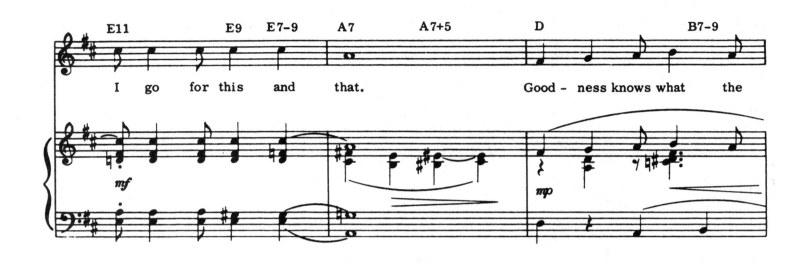

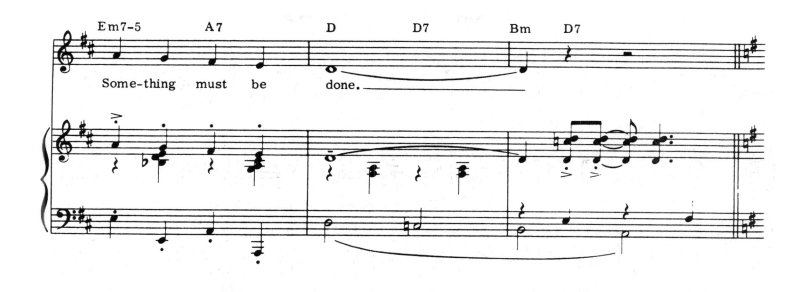

Let's Call the Whole Thing Off - 6 - 3

266

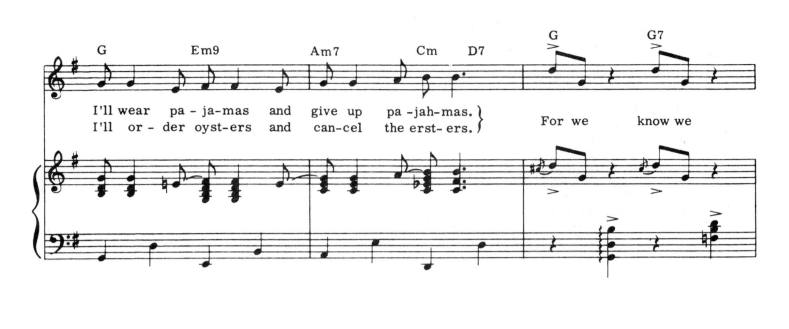

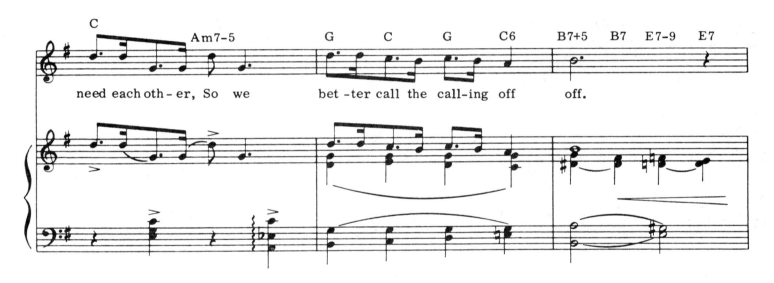

Let's Call the Whole Thing Off - 6 - 6

# Shall We Dance?

Music and Lyrics by
GEORGE GERSHWIN
and IRA GERSHWIN

Drop — that long face! - Come on, have — your fling!

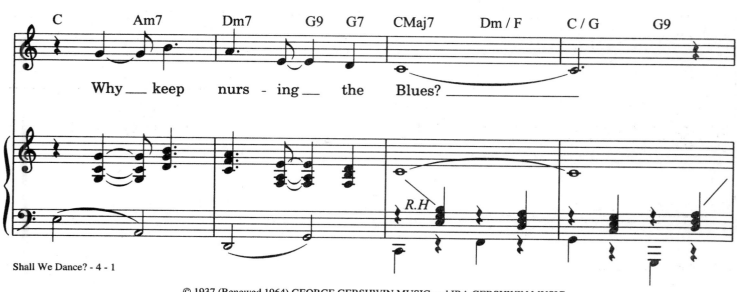

Why — keep nurs - ing — the Blues? _____

Shall We Dance? - 4 - 1

# SLAP THAT BASS

Music and Lyrics by
GEORGE GERSHWIN
and IRA GERSHWIN

Slap That Bass - 5 - 1

274

Slap That Bass - 5 - 2

# THEY ALL LAUGHED

Music and Lyrics by
GEORGE GERSHWIN
and IRA GERSHWIN

They All Laughed - 5 - 1

They told Mar-co-ni Wire-less was a pho-ney;
Ford and his Liz-zie Kept the laugh-ers bus-y;

It's the same old cry. They laughed at me_____ want - ing
That's how peo - ple are. They laughed at me_____ want - ing

you,_____ Said I was reach-ing for the moon; But
you,_____ Said it would be Hel - lo, Good - bye; But

oh, _____ You came through_ Now they'll have to change their tune.
oh, _____ You came through_ Now they're eat - ing hum - ble pie.

They All Laughed - 5 - 4

# THEY CAN'T TAKE THAT AWAY FROM ME

Music and Lyrics by
GEORGE GERSHWIN
and IRA GERSHWIN

Our ro-mance won't end on a sor-row-ful note, Though by to-mor-row you're

gone; The song is end-ed, but as the song-writ-er wrote, The

They Can't Take That Away From Me - 4 - 1

# WAKE UP, BROTHER, AND DANCE

Music and Lyrics by
GEORGE GERSHWIN
and IRA GERSHWIN

Crash those cym-bals!_____ Blow those trum-pets!_____

Mis- ter Maes- tro, start your beat!_____

# A FOGGY DAY

Music and Lyrics by
GEORGE GERSHWIN
and IRA GERSHWIN

Moderato

I was a strang-er in the cit-y.___ Out of town were the peo-ple I knew.

I had that feel-ing of self - pi-ty,___ What to do? What to do? What to do? The

A Foggy Day - 4 - 1

A Foggy Day - 4 - 4

# I Can't Be Bothered Now

Music and Lyrics by
GEORGE GERSHWIN
and IRA GERSHWIN

Mu-sic is the mag-ic that makes ev-'ry-thing sun-shin-y:

Danc-ing makes my trou-bles all seem ti-ny. _____ When I'm danc-ing

I don't care if this old world stops turn-ing, Or if my bank is

I Can't Be Bothered Now - 4 - 1

I Can't Be Bothered Now - 4 - 3

I Can't Be Bothered Now - 4 - 4

# THE JOLLY TAR AND THE MILK MAID

Music and Lyrics by
**GEORGE GERSHWIN**
and **IRA GERSHWIN**

302

The Jolly Tar and the Milk Maid - 4 - 2

The Jolly Tar and the Milk Maid - 4 - 4

# Nice Work If You Can Get It

Music and Lyrics by
GEORGE GERSHWIN
and IRA GERSHWIN

The man who on-ly lives for mak-ing mon-ey Lives a life that is-n't nec-es-sa-ri-ly sun-ny. Like-wise the man who works for fame,

Nice Work If You Can Get It - 5 - 1

Refrain: *(smoothly)*

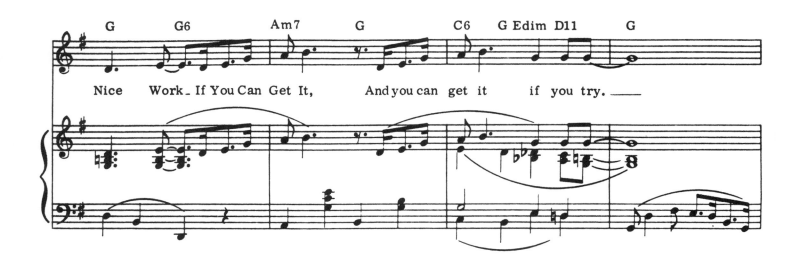

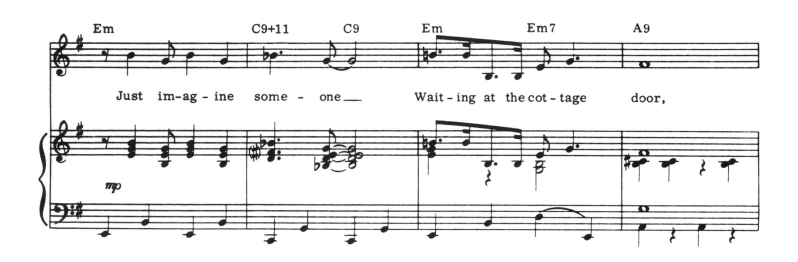

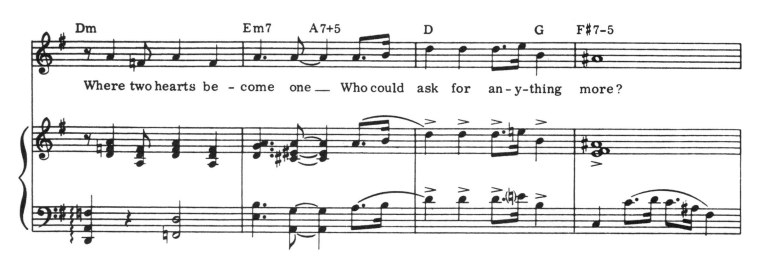

# STIFF UPPER LIP

Music and Lyrics by
GEORGE GERSHWIN
and IRA GERSHWIN

**Moderato (with humor)**

*Verse:*

What made good Queen Bess such a great suc-cess?

What made Well-ing-ton do what he did at Wa-ter-loo?

What makes ev-'ry Eng-lish-man a fight-er through and through? It

# Things Are Looking Up

Music and Lyrics by
**GEORGE GERSHWIN**
and **IRA GERSHWIN**

If I should sud-den-ly start to sing or stand on my head or an-y-thing, don't think that I've lost my sens - es; it's just that my hap-pi-ness fi-nal-ly com-menc-es._____ The long, long a-ges of

Things Are Looking Up - 4 - 1

Things Are Looking Up - 4 - 4

# I Love to Rhyme

Music and Lyrics by
GEORGE GERSHWIN
and IRA GERSHWIN

I Love to Rhyme - 4 - 1

I Love to Rhyme - 4 - 3

322

# I WAS DOING ALL RIGHT

Music and Lyrics by
GEORGE GERSHWIN
and IRA GERSHWIN

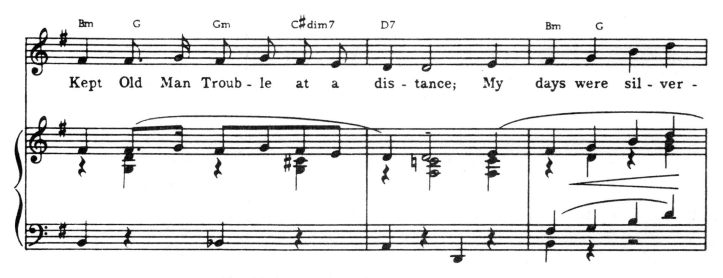

I Was Doing All Right - 4 - 1

I Was Doing All Right - 4 - 2

I Was Doing All Right - 4 - 4

# JUST ANOTHER RHUMBA

Music and Lyrics by
GEORGE GERSHWIN
and IRA GERSHWIN

Just Another Rhumba - 8 - 1

Just Another Rhumba - 8 - 3

# LOVE IS HERE TO STAY

Music and Lyrics by
**GEORGE GERSHWIN**
**and IRA GERSHWIN**

The more I read the pa- pers The less I com-pre - hend The

world and all its ca- pers And how it all will end. Noth-ing seems to be

Love Is Here to Stay - 4 - 1

# LOVE WALKED IN

Music and Lyrics by
GEORGE GERSHWIN
and IRA GERSHWIN

Love Walked In - 4 - 1

Time was stand-ing still, Noth-ing count-ed till There

came a knock-knock-knock-ing at the door. _____

**Refrain** *(slowly, with much expression)*

Love walked right in and drove the shad-ows a-

Love Walked In - 4 - 3

# Dawn of a New Day

Music and Lyrics by
**GEORGE GERSHWIN**
**and IRA GERSHWIN**

*Refrain:*

**Rhythmically**

Sound the brass! Roll the drum! To the world of to-mor-row we come!

See the sun through the gray, it's the dawn of a new day!

Here we come, young and old! Come to watch all the won-ders un-fold!

And the tune that we play is the dawn of a new day! Tell the

# AREN'T YOU KIND OF GLAD WE DID?

Music and Lyrics by
GEORGE GERSHWIN
and IRA GERSHWIN

Aren't You Kind of Glad We Did? - 4 - 1

# THE BACK BAY POLKA

Music and Lyrics by
GEORGE GERSHWIN
and IRA GERSHWIN

Give up the fond em-brace, Pass up that pret-ty face,
Don't speak the nak-ed truth. What's nak-ed is un-couth.
Some-where the fair-er sex Has curves that are con-vex,
On Bos-ton beans you dine, Then go to bed at nine.

You're of the hu-man race, But not in Bos-ton.
It may go in Du-luth But not in Bos-ton.
And girls don't all wear specs But not in Bos-ton.
You must-n't un-der-mine The town of Bos-ton.

The Back Bay Polka - 4 - 1

The Back Bay Polka - 4 - 2

354

The Back Bay Polka - 4 - 4

# Changing My Tune

Music and Lyrics by
GEORGE GERSHWIN
and IRA GERSHWIN

Refrain *(with a rocking rhythm)*

Cas - tles were crum - bling And day-dreams were tum-bling, De -
No more the feel - ing That my world is reel - ing, No

cem - ber was bat - tling with June. But on this bright af - ter -
fear - ing I'll fall in a swoon. Prob - lems are all pic - a -

noon, Guess I'll be chang - ing my tune.
yune, That's why I'm chang - ing my tune.

Kept on des - pair - ing Be - yond an - y car - ing If
Felt like a sail - or A - drift on a whal - er, A -

# FOR YOU, FOR ME, FOR EVERMORE

Music and Lyrics by
GEORGE GERSHWIN
and IRA GERSHWIN

Moderately

smoothly

Par - a - dise can-not re - fuse us, Nev - er such a hap - py pair!

Ev - 'ry-bod - y must ex - cuse us

For You, for Me, for Evermore - 4 - 1

For You, for Me, for Evermore - 4 - 3

For You, for Me, for Evermore - 4 - 4

# ONE, TWO, THREE

Music and Lyrics by
GEORGE GERSHWIN
and IRA GERSHWIN

One, Two, Three - 4 - 1

# All the Livelong Day
## (And The Long, Long Night)

Music and Lyrics by
GEORGE GERSHWIN
and IRA GERSHWIN

You've real-ly got me,___ I find I'm not me,___ The me I'd known in the past.___ You sim-ply stun me,___ Love has un-done me___ at last.___ From the be-gin-ning___ You had me

All the Livelong Day - 4 - 1

370

All the Livelong Day - 4 - 2

All the Livelong Day - 4 - 4

# I'M A POACHED EGG

Music and Lyrics by
GEORGE GERSHWIN
and IRA GERSHWIN

I'm a Poached Egg - 4 - 1

**Refrain** (*Brightly*)

1. I'm a poached egg with - out a piece of toast, York - shire
2. I'm Las Ve - gas with - out a slot ma - chine, I'm a

pud - ding with - out a beef to roast, I'm a haunt - ed house that
gyp - sy with - out a tam - bour - ine, I'm Na - po - le - on with -

has - n't got a ghost when I'm with - out you.___ I'm a
out a Jo - seph - ine when I'm with - out you.___ I'm a

mouse-trap with-out a piece of cheese, I'm Vi - en - na with -
let - ter with-out the right ad-dress, I'm a sand-wich with

out the Vi - en - nese, I'm Da Vin - ci with-out the Mo - na Lis', I'm
on - ly wa-ter-cress, I'm a ten - ant, the kind they dis - poss-ess, I'm

skies with - out blue.__ When you don't hang a - round I'm a kang-a-
bill with - out coo.__ There comes a time I don't know if I'm I

roo with - out a hop. When will you show me that as Ro - me -
or a wrest - ling match. The way you treat me, soon they'll greet me

*mf*  *slower and freely*

I'm a Poached Egg - 4 - 3

# SOPHIA

Music and Lyrics by
**GEORGE GERSHWIN**
and **IRA GERSHWIN**

Sophia - 5 - 1

# Ask Me Again

Music and Lyrics by
**GEORGE GERSHWIN**
**and IRA GERSHWIN**

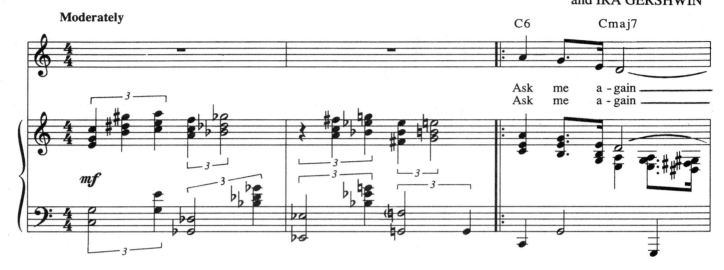

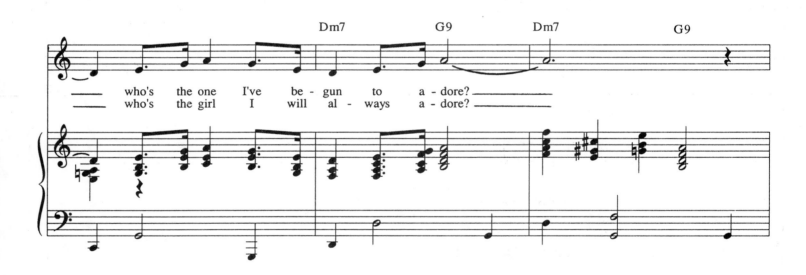

Ask Me Again - 3 - 1